Facts About the Zebra

By Lisa Strattin

© 2019 Lisa Strattin

FREE BOOK

FREE FOR ALL SUBSCRIBERS

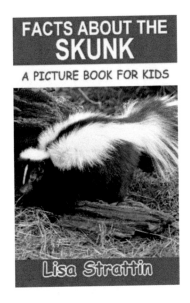

LisaStrattin.com/Subscribe-Here

BOX SET

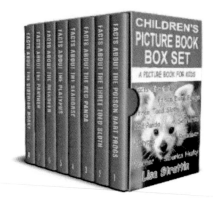

- FACTS ABOUT THE POISON DART FROGS
- FACTS ABOUT THE THREE TOED SLOTH
- FACTS ABOUT THE RED PANDA
- FACTS ABOUT THE SEAHORSE
- FACTS ABOUT THE PLATYPUS
- FACTS ABOUT THE REINDEER
- FACTS ABOUT THE PANTHER
- FACTS ABOUT THE SIBERIAN HUSKY

LisaStrattin.com/BookBundle

Facts for Kids Picture Books by Lisa Strattin

Little Blue Penguin, Vol 92

Chipmunk, Vol 5

Frilled Lizard, Vol 39

Blue and Gold Macaw, Vol 13

Poison Dart Frogs, Vol 50

Blue Tarantula, Vol 115

African Elephants, Vol 8

Amur Leopard, Vol 89

Sabre Tooth Tiger, Vol 167

Baboon, Vol 174

Sign Up for New Release Emails Here

LisaStrattin.com/subscribe-here

Contents

INTRODUCTION

The Zebra is a large species of equine that roams the grassy plains of sub-Saharan Africa. They are the largest wild horse with the most distinctive bodies patterned with white and black stripes, the exact stripe pattern being unique to each individual. There are three different in Africa: the Common Zebra (also known as the Plains Zebra and the Burchell's Zebra), the Grevy's Zebra (also known as the Imperial Zebra) and the Mountain Zebra.

Due to their free-roaming nature, the increasing human presence throughout the world has meant that they have been affected by the loss of their habitats throughout the natural range. They are so closely related to other horses and donkeys, that they have been able to breed. This animal is called a Zonkey or a Zorse, depending upon whether the animal is part horse or part donkey. However, like the mule, they cannot reproduce.

CHARACTERISTICS

Zebras are highly social animals that roam in herds ot provide protection from predators.. Their strong social bonds can make them very affectionate toward one another;, they have been observed grooming each other using their teeth. During the mating season, males will fight fiercely for the right to breed with females. They fight by rearing up on their back legs while they kick and bite one another.

The stripes of the Zebra remain a slight mystery to science. They were once thought to camouflage them into the natural light and shade of their surroundings, confusing predators, because when running as a herd, it is difficult to remain focused on any single animal!

The formation of the stripes on the rear end of the Zebra differs greatly between the three species; Common Zebras have horizontal stripes on its haunches while those of the Grevy's Zebra curve upwards. These patterns on their rear ends are thought to differ greatly in order that members of the same herd are able identify individuals at the front of the pack when running.

As with other male horses, zebra stallions are known to curl their top lips up, this is thought to heighten their sense of smell. This is called the "horse laugh" and proves vital for the male to be able to detect when a female is ready to mate.

APPEARANCE

Zebras are heavy-bodied animals that are designed for speed with long, slender legs and narrow hooves that help them to reach speeds of almost 25 miles per hour when running.

Like horses, they only have a single toe on each foot and they walk on the tip of it. This is protected by their tough hooves.. Zebras have long necks and heads; this means they can easily eat the grass on the ground. They have a mane that extends from their forehead, all along their back to the tail.

The pattern of stripes varies in the species with Grevy's and Mountain Zebras having narrower stripes and white undersides, while the Common Zebra has broad stripes that cover its entire body.

The Grevy's Zebra is not only the largest of the Zebra species but is also easily identifiable by its large, round ears.

LIFE STAGES

The Zebra is a relatively slow-developing mammal. Females are not able to breed until they are at least a few years old. After a gestation that can last for between 10 months and a year, the female gives birth to a single foal that is born with its stripes, mane and a little patch of hair in the middle of its tummy.

Zebra foals are able to stand right after birth, which is important so that they are able to run from predators. They are able to begin eating grass after a week and are totally weaned by the time they are 11 months old.

Young Zebras remain will with their mother until they around three years old. This is when the males leave their mother's herd to join an all-male bachelor group, while females stay with their mother. The bachelor groups begin to challenge the dominant stallions to try and take over the female harem during the mating season.

LIFE SPAN

Zebras live for an average of 20 to 30 years.

SIZE

Zebras can grow to be as long as 6.5 to 9 feet, weighing 500 to 900 pounds.

HABITAT

The Common Zebra is the most numerous and has the widest natural range throughout East Africa roaming the grassy plains. The Mountain Zebra is found grazing on the mountain grasslands of Southwest Africa, and the Grevy's Zebra is mostly confined to the arid grasslands and sub-desert steppes throughout Ethiopia, Somalia and in northern Kenya.

Although the Common Zebra has been least affected, all three species are considered at risk from population declines due to the loss of their natural habitats caused by increasing human activity in their home ranges.

DIET

The zebra is a herbivore. This means that it only eats plants in order to get the nutrition needed to survive. The majority of the Zebra's diet, in fact around 90%, is made up of a variety of different grasses along with other vegetation like leaves and buds making up the last 10%.

They use their front teeth to nibble on tough ends of grasses, and then they grind them up using flat molars along their cheeks. Unfortunately, grass has very little nutritional value, so zebras must spend more than half of their day grazing. Common Zebras are often seen drinking at water holes every day. But, since Grevy's Zebra and the Mountain Zebra live in drier, more arid regions, they often don't drink water for several days in a row.

ENEMIES

Zebras are large and powerful animals that can easily outrun many of its predators. They are preyed upon by lions, leopards, hyenas and African Wild Dogs, as well as a number of other large carnivores like the crocodiles, which will hunt them when they are crossing rivers or drinking.

Although their first instinct is to run away, zebras have been known to attack an animal that is threatening by kicking and biting. However, when danger is spotted, zebras warn one another and then run away as a tight herd. In this manner, they can either confuse or simply intimidate the attacker.

SUITABILITY AS PETS

Of course, zebras are not a good choice for a pet. If you want to see them, it is best to go to your city's zoo and watch them there.

COLOR ME

COLOR ME

COLOR ME

COLOR ME

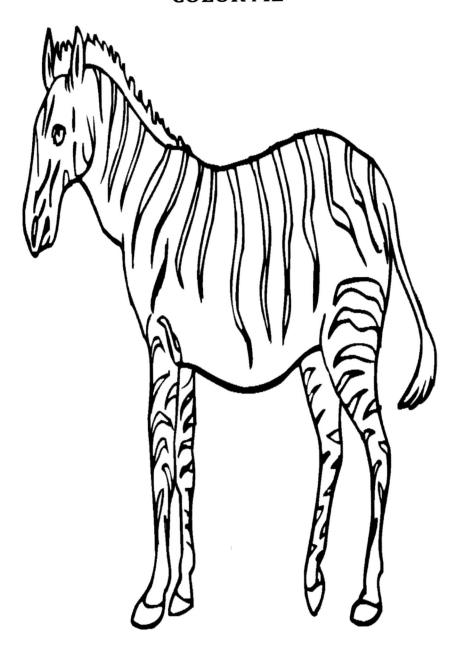

COLOR ME

COLOR ME

COLOR ME

COLOR ME

COLOR ME

COLOR ME

Please leave me a review here:

LisaStrattin.com/Review-Vol-202

For more Kindle Downloads Visit Lisa Strattin Author Page on Amazon Author Central

amazon.com/author/lisastrattin

To see upcoming titles, visit my website at LisaStrattin.com– most books available on Kindle!

LisaStrattin.com

FREE BOOK

FOR ALL SUBSCRIBERS – SIGN UP NOW

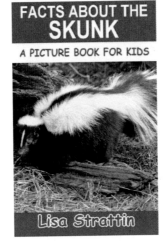

LisaStrattin.com/Subscribe-Here

LisaStrattin.com/Facebook

LisaStrattin.com/Youtube

Made in the USA
Middletown, DE
04 September 2023

37879948R00024